Jacoby, I think if
find time to attempt each
page, you will
find
your drawing ability will really
enlarge, 2023 Grammie

How to Draw
PIRATES

Captain, Crew, Ships and More

Barbara Soloff Levy

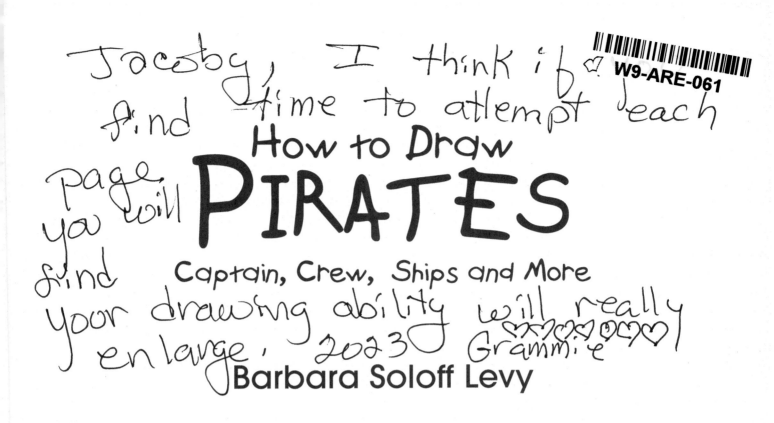

Dover Publications, Inc.
Mineola, New York

Bibliographical Note

How to Draw Pirates: Captain, Crew, Ships and More is a new work,
first published by Dover Publications, Inc., in 2008.

International Standard Book Number

ISBN-13: 978-0-486-46548-7
ISBN-10: 0-486-46548-9

Manufactured in the United States by LSC Communications
4500054922
www.doverpublications.com

How to Draw
PIRATES
Captain, Crew, Ships and More

Practice Page

Practice Page

6   Smug the Gold Hunter

Practice Page

Practice Page

Practice Page

Practice Page

Practice Page

Practice Page

Practice Page

Practice Page

Practice Page

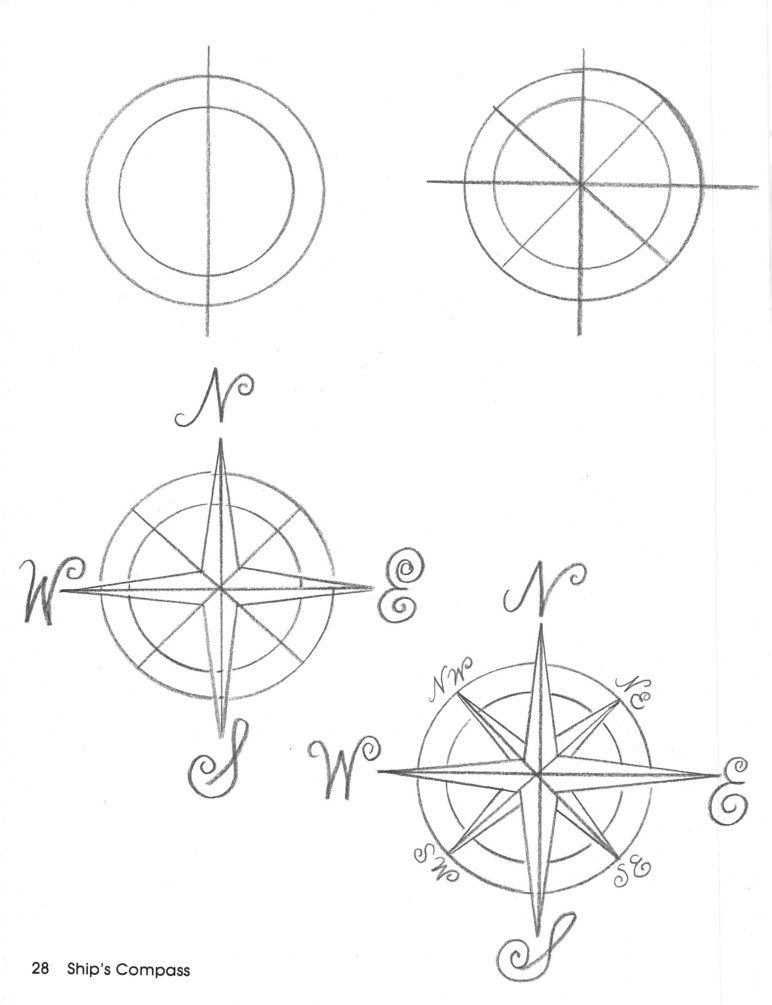

Practice Page

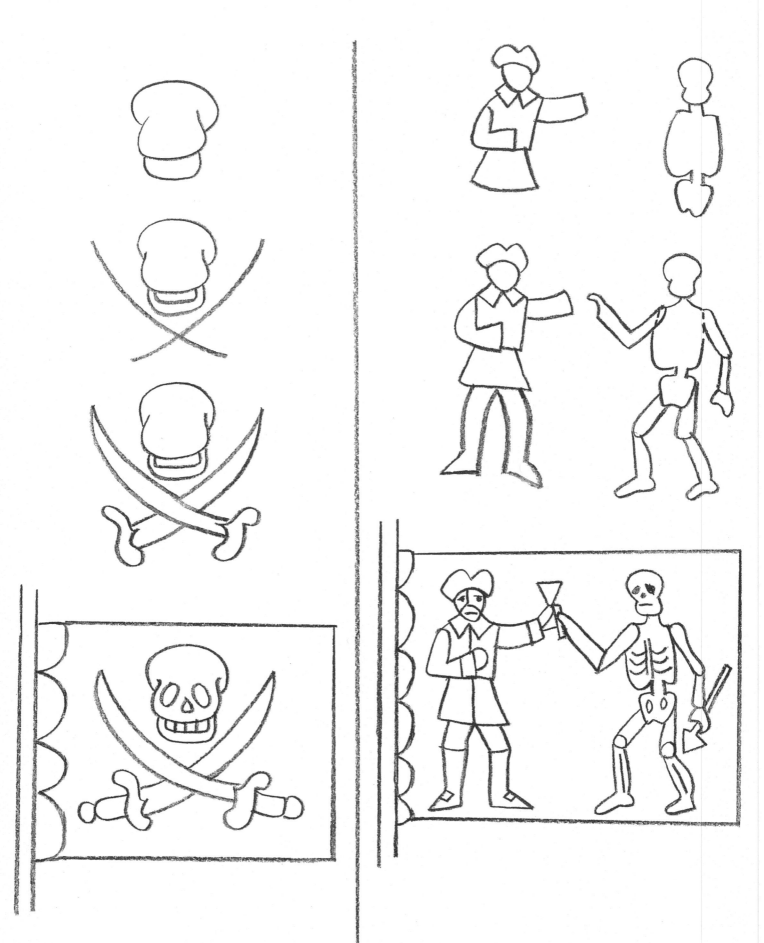

Practice Page

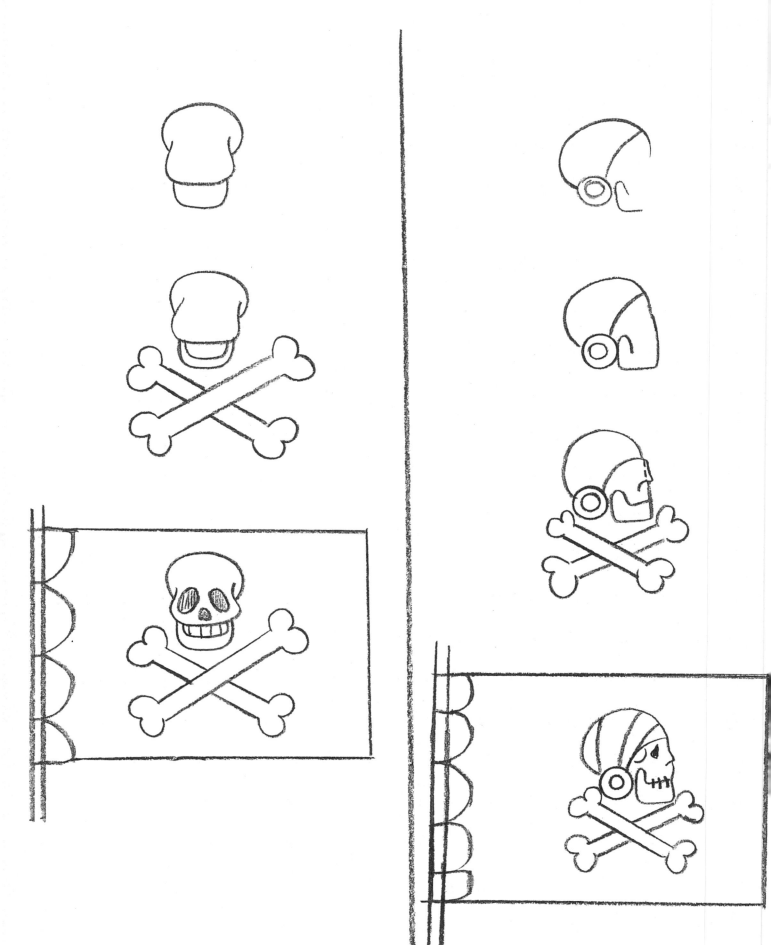

Practice Page

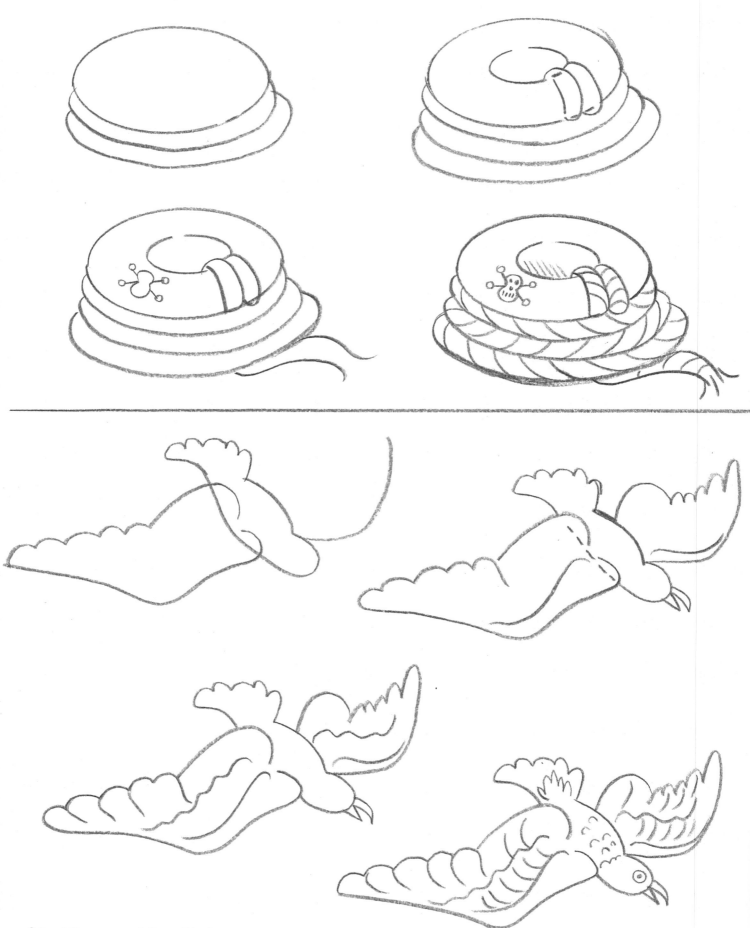

Practice Page

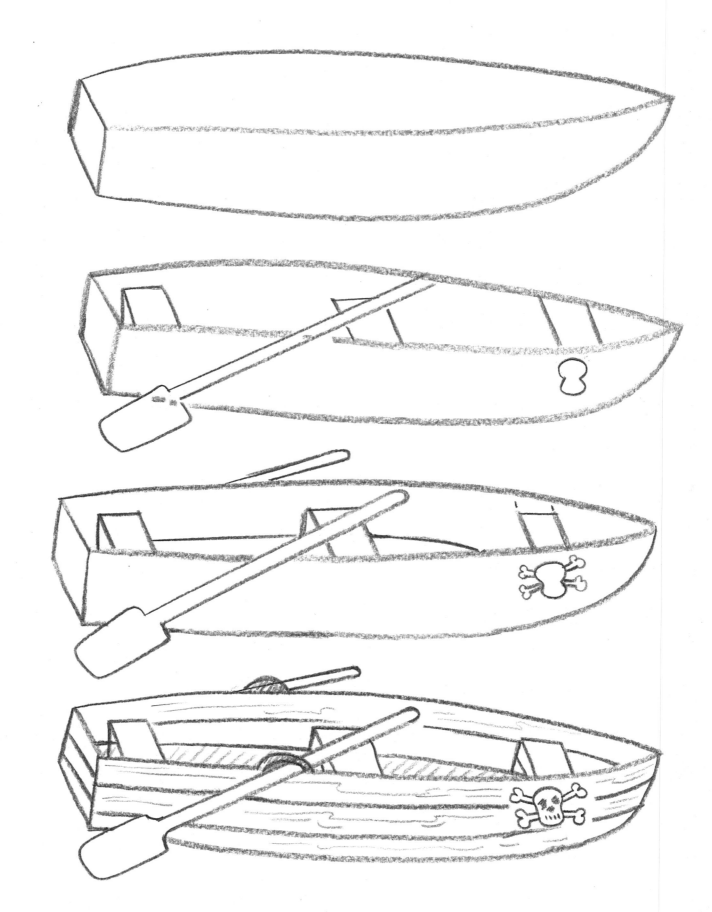

Practice Page

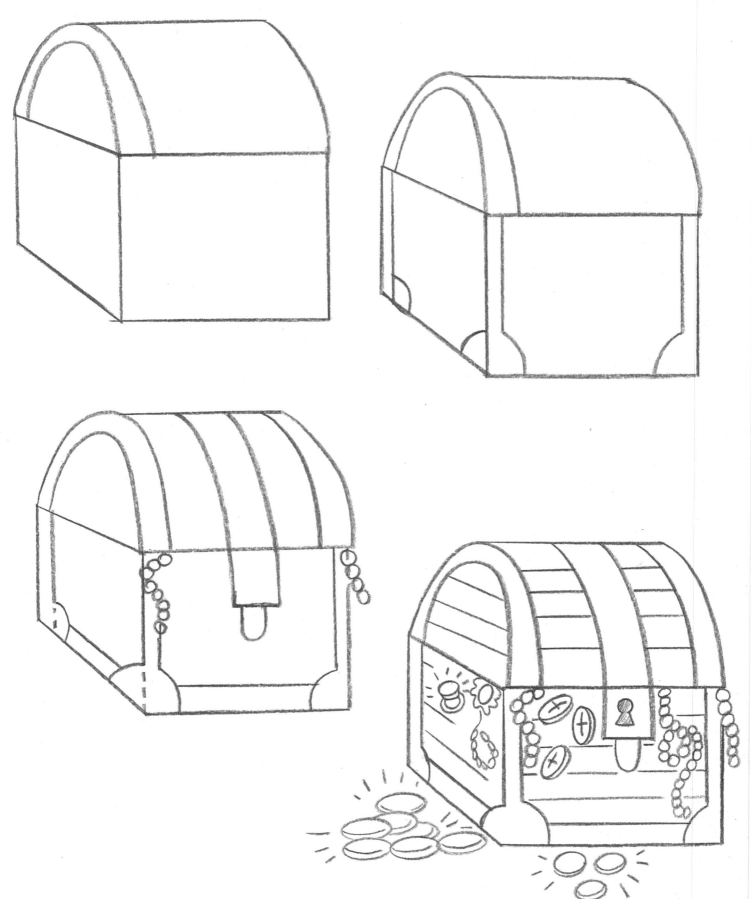

Practice Page

Practice Page

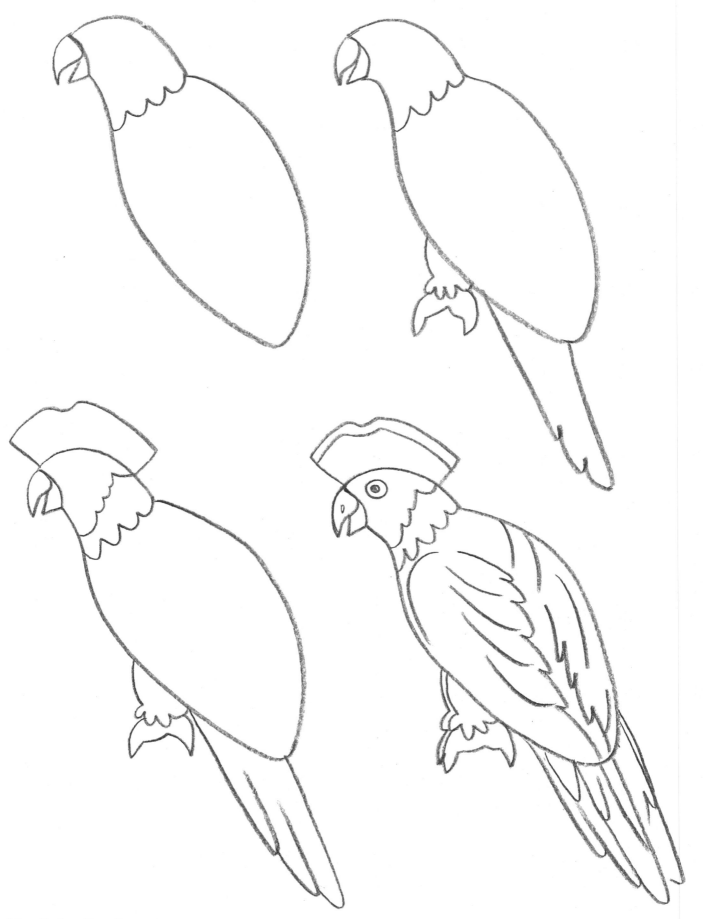

Practice Page

48   Water Barrel and Bucket

Practice Page

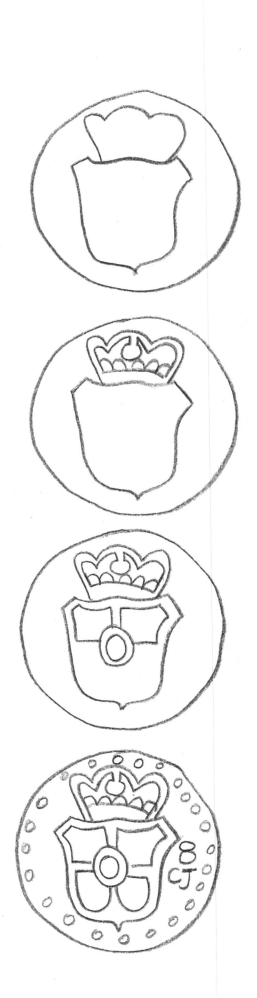

Practice Page

Practice Page

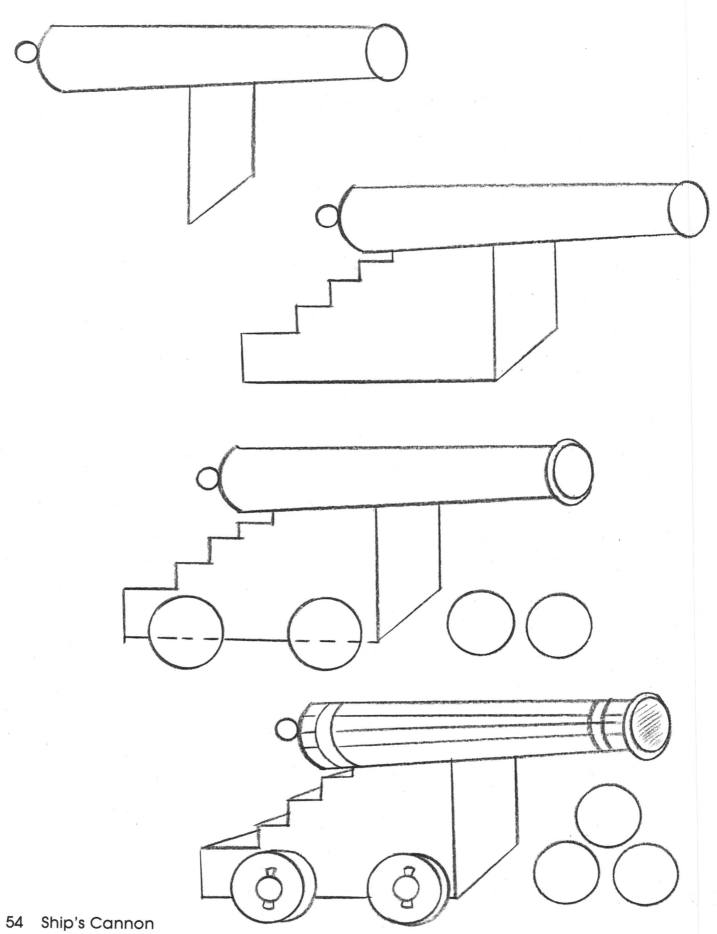

Practice Page

Island Tree and Flowers

Practice Page

Lizard, Seashell, Crab, Starfish

Practice Page